Reptile World
Rattlesnakes

by Vanessa Black

Bullfrog Books

Ideas for Parents and Teachers

Bullfrog Books let children practice reading informational text at the earliest reading levels. Repetition, familiar words, and photo labels support early readers.

Before Reading

- Discuss the cover photo. What does it tell them?
- Look at the picture glossary together. Read and discuss the words.

Read the Book

- "Walk" through the book and look at the photos. Let the child ask questions. Point out the photo labels.
- Read the book to the child, or have him or her read independently.

After Reading

- Prompt the child to think more. Ask: Have you ever seen a rattlesnake? Was it wild or in a zoo? Did you hear its rattle?

Bullfrog Books are published by Jump!
5357 Penn Avenue South
Minneapolis, MN 55419
www.jumplibrary.com

Library of Congress Cataloging-in-Publication Data

Names: Black, Vanessa, author.
Title: Rattlesnakes / by Vanessa Black.
Other titles: Bullfrog books. Reptile world.
Description: Minneapolis, MN: Bullfrog Books, [2017]
Series: Reptile world
Audience: Ages 5–8. | Audience: K to grade 3.
Includes index.
Identifiers: LCCN 2016002936
ISBN 9781620313848 (hardcover: alk. paper)
Subjects: LCSH: Rattlesnakes—Juvenile literature.
Classification: LCC QL666.O69 B53 2017
DDC 597.96/38—dc23
LC record available at http://lccn.loc.gov/2016002936

Editor: Jenny Fretland VanVoorst
Series Designer: Ellen Huber
Book Designer: Lindaanne Donohoe
Photo Researcher: Lindaanne Donohoe

Photo Credits: Alamy, 18–19, 23tr; Biosphoto, 9; Corbis, 5, 14, 16–17, 23tl; Getty Images, 20–21; Shutterstock, cover, 3, 4, 6, 6–7, 8, 10–11, 15, 22, 23bl, 24; ThinkStock, 1, 12–13, 23br.

Printed in the United States of America at Corporate Graphics in North Mankato, Minnesota.

Table of Contents

Back Off!

A rattlesnake
lies in the sun.

He is cold-blooded.
He needs the sun
to get warm.

Look!
An owl.
She is hungry.
She flies down.

The snake shakes his tail.
It rattles.

Back off!

The owl flies away.

A rattle is not dangerous.

But venom is.

Look!

He has fangs.

fangs

13

Here is a rat.

The snake bites.

venom

Venom comes out of his fangs.

The rat dies.

The snake eats.

He will not eat again
for two weeks.

Look!

A rattlesnake
is shedding.

She sheds two to three times a year.

Each time she grows a new ring on her rattle.

rattle

Parts of a Rattlesnake

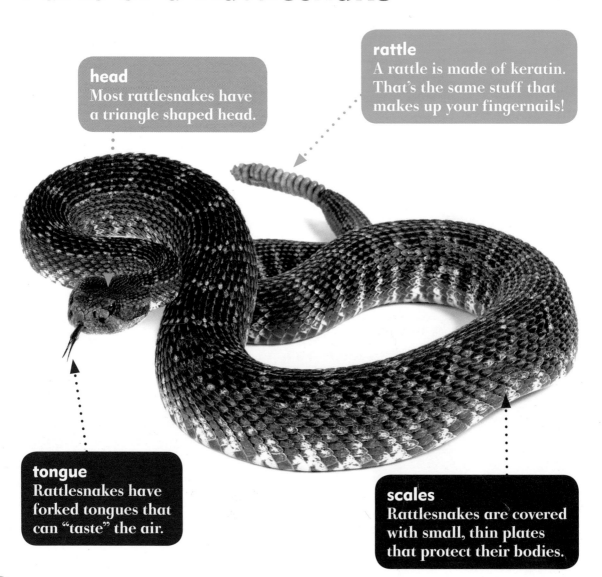

head
Most rattlesnakes have a triangle shaped head.

rattle
A rattle is made of keratin. That's the same stuff that makes up your fingernails!

tongue
Rattlesnakes have forked tongues that can "taste" the air.

scales
Rattlesnakes are covered with small, thin plates that protect their bodies.

Picture Glossary

cold-blooded
Animals that have the same temperature as their environment.

shedding
When a snake's skin comes off.

fangs
Long front teeth; rattlesnakes have hollow fangs that can inject venom.

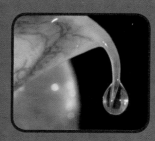
venom
Poison.

Index

To Learn More

Learning more is as easy as 1, 2, 3.

1) Go to www.factsurfer.com

2) Enter "rattlesnakes" into the search box.

3) Click the "Surf" button to see a list of websites.

With factsurfer.com, finding more information is just a click away.